Coming Soon

Babette's Bubble-Wrap Couture®
Active-Adult Misadventures with a Gracefully-Challenged Fashionista!

Babette's Bubble-Wrap Couture®
World-Wide Misadventures with a Gracefully-Challenged Fashionista!

Babette's Bubble-Wrap Couture®
Misadventures with a Gracefully-Challenged Dog Lover!

Babette's Bubble-Wrap Couture®

Babette's Bubble-Wrap Couture®

Seasonal Misadventures with a Gracefully-Challenged Fashionista!

Babette Bersch

Copyright 2023 by Barbara Bersch

All rights reserved.
This book or any portion thereof may not be reproduced or used in any manner whatsoever without the express written permission of the publisher except for the use of brief quotations in a book review.

First Printing 2023
ISBN 979-8-218-29191-4

It took a "Village" to get me back on my feet and I don't think it's possible to even come close to being able to thank everyone involved in saving my life!

A very special thank you to all the first responders and enormous medical teams. You literally give the gift of life.

To the Helicopter Pilot: Thank you for the ride and I forgive you for losing my paperwork...LOL...#JaneDoe

To Donna and Jeff: Thank you for answering your door at 1:30 AM, going with me to the hospital, saving Wilson and helping nurse me back to good health!

Hugs and much love to my friends and neighbors who helped me heal.

To my brother, Gary: You dropped everything to come to my side, stay by my side, nurse me back to good health and managed to still torture me a little bit! Your love and care can never be repaid and will never be forgotten!

To my husband John: What can I say? You were there every moment with me through the toughest times of my life! I feel your love everyday and appreciate your unwavering support! Forever yours!

Last but not least...to God: Your miracles have not been lost on me and have definitely opened my eyes to both the fragility and preciousness of life! Thank you for loving me!

I admit that I'm clumsy and awkward...

and a little bit accident prone.

I've been injured in all kinds of settings...

the slopes, pumpkin patch...

and at home!

My look says I own lots of diamonds...

Collect crystal, antiques and the like.

My elegance will never elude me...

Even when fishing or riding my bike.

Couple my sense of adventure...

With the refined Fashionista within...

Yes, I love to wear designer labels...

and those hospital gowns are a **SIN**!

My goal moving forward is simple...

I'll stay lovely and keep my allure...

While keeping my body protected...

in my unique "BUBBLE-WRAP COUTURE"!

First it's a trip to the mountains...

a holiday stay at the lodge...

Decorating the tree...

And then off to ski...

Though Black Diamonds...

I needed to dodge!

My skills aren't the best,

but to me it's no trouble...

'Cause my Ski-Bunny suit's made of BUBBLE!

Spring has arrived!

There are flowers to plant...

and rain shower puddles to jump in!

Then I skid through the mud...

and come down with a thud!

My knees start to buckle,

but my laughter just doubles...

'Cause my raincoat is made out of BUBBLES!

It's summer again and the sun's shining bright...

We finally have much warmer weather!

I'm looking real cool and jump into the pool...

Boy, this day couldn't get any better!

Then I slip on the deck...

Almost cracking my neck...

and the life-guard was there on the double!

I said, "I'm OK"...

and went on my way...

in my swimsuit that's made out of BUBBLE!

Fall's in the air...

and the leaves are bright colors...

I'm picking out pumpkins to carve!

As the wind starts to whip, on a pumpkin I trip and land onto my backside quite hard!

I quickly stand up and I'm laughing in hoots…

'Cause the BUBBLES that cover…

my sweater and boots…

kept me safe…

in my pumpkin pursuits!

As the seasons unfold...

My bold story will be told...

I'm a girl who is lacking in grace!

Whether Winter or Spring...

You'll be sure to find me...

Tripping on nothing or...

wearing a brace!

Accidents occuring in Summer and Fall...

Some of them big...

And some of them small...

I'm sure to have mishaps and troubles!

But I'll look my best...

'Cause I will be dressed...

in my fashions that are...

Made out of BUBBLES!

The Happy & Fashionable End

www.ingramcontent.com/pod-product-compliance
Lightning Source LLC
Chambersburg PA
CBRC102029050526
44107CB00111B/1276